My Girl

Bill Combs

xulon
PRESS

Copyright © 2008 by Bill Combs

My Girl
by Bill Combs

Printed in the United States of America

ISBN 978-1-60477-590-7

All rights reserved solely by the author. The author guarantees all contents are original and do not infringe upon the legal rights of any other person or work. No part of this book may be reproduced in any form without the permission of the author. The views expressed in this book are not necessarily those of the publisher.

Unless otherwise indicated, Bible quotations are taken from the New International Version of the Bible. Copyright © 1973, 1978, 1984 by the International Bible Society. Used by permission of Zondervan Publishing House.

www.xulonpress.com

Dedication

This book is dedicated to everybody who's lost a loved one, but especially to Jeanette and Annie, two southern American women of strong heart and character, humble in attitude, and tenacious in spirit who moved through life with the sweet spirit of God, touching others with compassion, and facing death with courage and faith. This is for them, the women like them and the men who see how truly wonderful they are.

There's no greater gift God can give to a man than a good wife.

Also by Bill Combs

God Is Alive

Contents

Forward xi

Jeanette 17

Annie 59

Epilogue 113

Forward

They say you don't know what you have till it's gone. Well, that may be true for some, but I knew that my cup ran over every time she smiled. My blessing was a plain-spoken country girl named Annie that lit up every room she ever walked into.

Four years into our marriage I got a call from Bobby Nicholson who wanted me to write a book about his wife that had passed away the previous year. At the time, Annie was very sick. Having my hands full, I told Bobby I just couldn't do it then but I'd try to later. He'd call about once a month to check on her. Annie died that November.

That's been three years ago. Bobby persisted in wanting his Jeanette's story told. We discussed it further and I felt that we weren't the only grieving widowers around and we should see if there were other men that wanted their wives' stories told. I spoke to several men, put ads in the paper and sent letters to about a dozen area pastors to see if they had any interested members.

We wanted six or seven guys to add to this, to tell their wives' stories. For one reason or another, it's just Bobby and me. For over two years now, he's been sending me an envelope a month telling Jeanette's story. We've only met once. I don't know if he still visits her grave as often as he did. He used to go see her four or five times a day. From his sheer dedication to telling her story, I know he loved her very much. Sadly, I know all too well how he feels.

Grief and love are powerful feelings. I think it's fair to say that most men hold their feelings in. I guess the feelings Bobby had for Jeanette and I had for Annie are just too big to be held in.

Thrust into a fraternity we didn't choose to join, we've come together not to say what wonderful fellows we are, but just to simply say "Thanks" to Him from whom all blessings flow and gave us the time we had with these wonderful women we had the privilege to know and to love.

This isn't a book that wallows in our collective or singular grief. This is a humble, heartfelt tribute to two thoroughly wonderful women, how we met them, why we loved them and how each in their own sweet way, made us better men. The world they touched was better for them having walked in it. Nobody famous, these are just everyday girls-next-door, that lived with quiet strength, courage, compassion and faith. They didn't grace the cover of magazines but women such as these men dream about. From women cut from this cloth, families are raised, communities are built, jobs get done, faith is displayed, people learn, and yes, even nations are better off.

They say you've got to take the bitter with the sweet. We feel with these sweet girls we've already had a glimpse of heaven. Even knowing that to be immersed in this temporary bliss meant one day having to drink down the bitterness of despair, of having to carry on without her; even knowing that the two are coupled, one with the other inextricably linked…to not know her, meaning without having to be without her later… we both agree. She's worth it. Set'em up again. If not hurting like this means not loving her, then we'll take it. We'll take it and we'll do the best we can. That's what He wants and that's what she wants. The answers come not from fighting against God, but in trusting Him. Knowing that the same loving God that brought us the delight of our eyes, that saw our first kiss even before we were

My Girl

made, He has ordained it so. Despite the tears of this world we'll be reunited.

We've had our glimpses of heaven, each individually wrapped in the perfect girl for us. It wouldn't be heaven without them there. To that goal we press on. These stories we tell simply to thank God for blessing us so perfectly and to thank these wonderful women for just being themselves.

Jeanette

Jeanette
(As told by Bobby Nicholson)

In those days, money was hard to come by. Gasoline was a quarter a gallon and a loaf of bread was eleven cents. For six dollars you could buy a week's worth of groceries but you were lucky to make fifty cents to a dollar a day. It was November of 1954 and I was home on a thirty-day leave from Korea.

I went to visit a schoolmate, James, in Jackson, Tennessee. His family was poor like mine, living in a row of shotgun houses. They were wooden houses with cracks between the boards big enough to toss a cat through. Freezing in winter and boiling in summer, there was no electricity or running water. So, light came by coal oil lamps and water came from the creek. To wash clothes folks used a rub board and a water basin.

I was standing in the front door of James' house ready to go back home when I saw her. She was in her backyard washing clothes. I asked James who that pretty girl was. He told me she was Jeanette, his neighbor, the oldest of six kids. So I went over and told her who I was and started talking to her. She told me all about her family. When the laundry was done she invited me in to meet them. I met her brothers and sisters and her mother. Her mother was a wonderful person. She depended on Jeanette since she was the oldest, to help out around the house. Since Jeanette had finished school she was able to do that.

I asked her mother if it would be OK to take Jeanette to the movies. She said yes, but I'd have to check with her father. He worked for the state highway department and was still at work. They invited me to stay for supper so I waited for him to come home. I was getting scared about asking him since we'd never met. I'd never asked a girl's mother or father if I could court her so this was a first for me. He came in and was washing up. He was a big man. Her mother was real nice about it. She'd already told him and said she thought I was nice. So there I was sitting across from him so scared I was at a loss for words. He looked at me and asked if I wanted to date his daughter. I said yes and he told me we'd talk in the living room after supper.

We sat across from each other. He said that he had strict rules for all his children but if he let me court Jeanette I had to understand the rules applied to her as well. She had to be home by eleven or she'd be grounded for three days. We talked for a long time that night. He asked me about the war. I told him I was with the 25th division in Korea but I really didn't want to talk about it. I looked in the kitchen and saw Jeanette with a big smile on her face. I guess she knew he was going to say yes. I went out and sat on their front porch and it wasn't too long before she came out and sat down right beside me. I said to myself, "I have a girlfriend now."

I came back and took her out the next day. She asked if I was out of the Army. I told her I'd served seventeen months in combat in Korea but I was on a thirty-day leave. I was thinking about re-enlisting for fifteen years but all I knew then was that I was going to be home again during Christmas and had to report to Fort Hood in Texas by January 14th to serve one more year.

I got up the nerve and held her hand. She told me she worked at the Salvation Army store. I really believe this is where she learned to love and respect people. A bad tornado had come through in 1953 and almost wiped Henderson out, about thirty miles away.

She told me how the Red Cross and Salvation Army had gone in to help. She'd seen so many bodies. I reckon this really put it into her heart to help people.

She asked me where I went to church. I hadn't been to church since I was about twelve, so she invited me to go with her and her mother that Sunday. We went to the Salvation Army church. It was a big building. I saw Jeanette and her mother bow their heads and so I did too. After the service she introduced me to the Salvation Army captain. I can't remember his name. That's been fifty years ago, but he told me what a wonderful girl Jeanette was, how she'd helped everyone in Henderson and how she had a servant's heart. She'd been teaching the children in Sunday school. He wished us well and told us that we should both love God.

After hearing all his kind words and seeing the type of person she was I felt real good about her. So we drove home, with Jeanette in front with me, and her mother in the back. Her mother started asking about my family. I told her I was an only child. I'd lost my mother to breast cancer when I was seven. They came to school and told me my mother had died. My Dad raised me till I was eighteen. I got drafted, pulled two years and then re-enlisted for four more, but I wasn't real sure if I was going to stay longer than that.

I asked if I could take Jeanette to visit my Dad. I hadn't seen him in over three years. So the next day I picked her up in my 1953 Chevrolet Bel-Air. There I was, at home with a new car and a good-looking girlfriend. I knew God was smiling down on me.

We drove up and Dad was out front to meet us. We went in and sat and talked. Those two hit it off right from the start. She wanted to know how my folks had met. Dad told her how he'd grown up on a farm in Conway, Arkansas. He came to Tennessee and met my Mom who was also a farm girl. They fell in love and got married. My Mom died in 1937. Dad stayed on their farm until he died of cancer in 1968.

So, we agreed to drive into Jackson. The depression and WWII had hit that area hard. Dad said that the chamber of commerce wouldn't allow any factories in and the place really hadn't changed much. He was right. I'd fought in that dirty war overseas and came home to a town that hadn't changed at all. I couldn't understand it and it made me a little bitter. Jeanette said that we should trust God and as long as you're nice to others they'll be nice back to you. After a couple of hours we drove Dad back home. Dad was handicapped but he still worked hard. Those two really liked each other.

We went to the movies and bowling. We went to church every Sunday we could. I was going to have to leave for Fort Hood soon. We talked about our lives and what we'd learned from our parents. Hard work and honest values were our heritage. We kissed but didn't go any further.

Christmas came and I sure enjoyed being with her and her family. I said goodbye to my Dad, telling him I'd let him know I got to Fort Hood all right. I went to say goodbye to Jeanette. She asked if I'd take her to pick up her dry cleaning. We did and returned to her house. She went inside leaving her clothes in the back and walked out with a suitcase.

She was going with me. I told her she couldn't. I didn't even know if the Army was going to station me in Texas or where. We argued and she didn't budge. I went in and talked to her mother. Her mother said Jeanette had made up her mind.

Jeanette and I left Jackson on January 8, 1955 for the 2000-mile trip to Fort Hood. Back then it was a two-lane highway all the way. We made it into Arkansas and she asked me if I loved her. I said that

I did. Then she asked if I'd marry her. I said that I would, I just hadn't counted on it so fast.

Hope, Arkansas was the next town we came to. We were married by the very nice judge there. From there we went through Fort Smith and then on to Texas. We stopped in Waco. I had to be on base by eight the next morning. I had to find out my assignment, get her a base pass and settle in.

I was assigned to a tank battalion of the third armored division. I manned a sixty- caliber machine gun on the tank. We had a real problem finding housing. There were so many service families there and everything close was rented up. We had to go eighty-four miles back to Waco to find an apartment. The landlady was real nice. She and Jeanette got along great. I had to work most weekends so they went to church together. I went when I could.

Jeanette never missed a Sunday. She wound up teaching a children's Sunday school class. After about six or seven months she told me she'd like to work at the base hospital. I knew better than to argue. She rode in with me one day and applied for the job. About a month later a letter came saying she'd been accepted. She was so tickled to be working where I did. So, we drove together the eighty-four miles each way from Waco to Fort Hood everyday. She always told me to believe in myself and trust God. She was right. She got that hospital job and still taught Sunday school.

I started having flashbacks of combat back in Korea. It would hit me anytime day or night. It was some of the worst mountains you've ever seen over there. We started naming them, Old Baldy and Pork Chop Hill. The snow was waist-deep in places and the supply trucks had a hard time getting through. Many times, we weren't sure if we were going to run out of ammo and food. There was a good friend of mine, named William Waldrop from North Carolina who was with me over there. We'd gotten orders from our captain that we had to dig in and hold that hill at all costs. My squad had two .30 caliber machine guns on the left and one on the right. We had a couple of BAR's and nine more riflemen with some extra men also. We knew they'd hit us at dawn. All through the night, I kept thinking of my buddies in the squad, especially William. We were expecting 500 Red Chinese but the daylight revealed at least three times that. Men were falling all around me, then they started dropping mortar rounds on us. One came in right on top of us. I got it in the back and the legs. My buddy got hit pretty bad in the legs. They called in a copter and got us to the field hospital. I don't know how he came out. Seems like we'd lose a hill one day, re-take it the next, only to lose it again the next.

I remember one weekend in April or May while Jeanette and I were at Fort Hood. I had drawn guard duty that weekend. Friday night me, and three of my men decided to let loose and drank way too much. I didn't get in until midnight or one that night and didn't wake up until around noon the next day. I got up with one whopper of a hangover. Not looking forward to facing Jeanette, I eased into the kitchen. My head was splitting. She had fresh coffee on and handed me a cup with some aspirin. She sat down beside me and I knew I was in trouble. I let her do the talking. This was the first time she'd ever been angry with me. I tried to answer all her questions the best I knew how, but most of them there wasn't any answer to, except I had done something stupid and wrong. She told me straight out she wasn't having it. She intended to leave me and go back home. She went into the bedroom. Some of her clothes were already packed. I followed her in there and asked her if she'd at least stay until I got off guard duty. She asked me why she should. I told her that I thought everybody deserved a second chance. That wasn't good enough.

My Girl

I told her that I loved her. She was the only girlfriend I'd ever had. When I was younger I had to help my Dad on the farm. I was too busy working. I never had time to have a girlfriend until her. I loved her and I needed her. She never said a word.

As I got ready to leave she hugged me and said she'd be there when I got home. As I drove the eighty-four miles in on that two-lane road, I thought about how I'd messed up. I got my men placed and went into the mess hall for some coffee. Sgt. Hood was in there. He was one stripe above me and sized me up pretty quick. He asked me why I'd tied one on. I told him maybe my mind was on what had happened over there, seeing my good friend William go down and all. He told me he'd been over there and had flashbacks too, but we couldn't let them damage our relationships with our families. He told me that I should go to church with Jeanette in the morning and I should ask forgiveness and God's help. He was right.

I got back and Jeanette and I talked. She'd told my Dad what I'd done. I promised her I'd never do it again. We went to church and I prayed for forgiveness. It felt good because I knew we got everything squared away.

I'll always appreciate the sound advice I got from Sgt. Hood. The Lord uses people to help you. There was a young soldier stationed with me in Germany named Eugene Chandler. He was always reading his Bible and invited me to go to church with him. I always had an excuse to do something else. I guess God puts people in your life to draw you closer. We were both headed for Korea but I never saw him again.

Jeanette was real supportive of me. I think her time at the base hospital gave her some insight into what soldiers have to live with. She suggested we go talk to our pastor. He was a friendly, middle-aged man. He was always helpful and good to us. Hearing him preach the gospel always lifted our spirits and gave us hope.

Time was coming to decide on re-enlistment. She didn't want me to, but made it clear it was my decision. The Army offered me another stripe if I'd "re-up" for fifteen years. I began hearing about Vietnam. I'd been wounded in Korea and was single back then. Now I had a wonderful wife that God had blessed me with and I'd seen war. She didn't pressure me but I knew in my heart I belonged with her. I'd given the Army six years. I made up my mind to do the right thing. We wrote to our families telling them we were coming back home.

Jeanette and I met a lot of nice people at Fort Hood and in Waco. She got six or seven awards from the base hospital for being such a good employee and got one from the church too. She helped our landlady a lot. They were really close friends. Jeanette worked at the Salvation Army in Waco on her days off. She loved people and loved helping them. I remember all those early mornings. We'd have to be up by four to make it to the base by seven. We'd listen to a country music show out of Del Rio on the radio. It was different than today's music. You could actually understand what they were saying.

On the afternoon drive back we'd listen to a gospel program out of Waco. They'd play "Peace in the Valley" and "The Old Rugged Cross". You don't hear shows like that much anymore either. Those drives gave us time together and were good for us. We never argued or fussed. If we had a problem we'd talk it out and work it out.

She loved children. At the Salvation Army store lots of kids would come in with their folks needing clothes and shoes and food. Folks back then had seen the hard times of the Depression and the rationing of sugar, coffee, tires and gas during World War II. America in 1955 still had plenty of poor people. I'd go and help out when I was off the base. It made me feel good but Jeanette thrived on it.

It was hard to say goodbye to our pastor and all our friends on the base and in Waco. Of course at the base hospital they hated to see Jeanette go and told me what a fine young woman she was.

So we got in our Chevy and headed back home. We were a little scared. The Army was all I'd known for the last five or six years. We got into Jackson around midnight the next day. We stayed with Jeanette's parents for what we thought would be two weeks. We applied for jobs all over town. There was a lumberyard, a meat-packing plant and a cotton mill. Nobody was hiring. We'd keep checking back but with no luck. The cotton mill said they might have some openings in six months to a year. We started applying all over the county. I even went to the Veterans Affairs office, but they didn't help.

We knew we had to make it on our own. We didn't want to live off our families. My uncles Oliver and Sam had decorating businesses in town and I went to them asking for a job. They were my mother's brothers and good Christian men. They wouldn't tolerate drinkin' or cussin'. I didn't drink but I had cussed some during the war.

They put me on. I'd work two weeks for one then two weeks for the other. I never had hung wallpaper or swung a paintbrush so I had a lot to learn. Jeanette helped her Dad. He was still working for the state. On his off days he'd cut grass and pick up odd jobs. She'd help and he'd give her half what he was paid. Times were tough as our country was still trying to heal after two wars.

I worked with my uncles for about four years. Jeanette was right in there with me. We hung wallpaper, painted and built porches. I got a part-time job making $1.25 an hour working three days a week making attic stairs. She had a job in a restaurant. She'd usually bring home more in tips than the $1.25 an hour she was making. I'd get off at three and go to cutting lawns till dark, then we'd go home to eat. After supper, we'd paint houses till twelve or one. For years we'd pick up any job we could. We picked cotton, chopped cotton and picked strawberries for a nickel a quart. I drove tractors and combines. Our rent was $6 a week. Our light bill was $13 a month and gasoline was 25 cents a gallon. We lived beside my aunt and uncle. She and Jeanette got along fine and helped each other out a lot.

Our first son, Robert, was born in January of 1956. When Jeanette was ready to go back to work my aunt and uncle would babysit for us. I think they and my Dad spoiled him; they loved him so much. Having an extra mouth to feed, she ran an ad in the paper offering to do laundry and ironing. That went well and brought in needed extra money.

As the years passed God blessed us with two more sons, Curtis, born in April of 1959 and Chris, born in November of 1968. I remember one day Jeanette was home on her day off. She was cleaning house. She had a what-not stand in the corner of the living room and as she was dusting it she saw most of the pieces had been broken and glued back together. When I got home we called the three boys in. Jeanette asked for my belt. The boys remained loyally silent for a while then we found out that the two older boys had been wrestling in the living room while Chris, the youngest, served as a lookout. In the process of their recreation they'd knocked over the stand and broken practically everything on it. We had a long talk with them about how hard we had to work to give them a nice home, stressing the value of hard work, not the material things. We disciplined our boys like our fathers had disciplined us. We had rules in our home. It was our job to teach our sons right and wrong and we did our best.

In 1974 Jeanette decided to go to college to become an R.N. She applied for a grant and got it. So for four years she worked during the day and went to college at night. My aunt and her mother helped out a lot and she did it. Unable to find nursing work in Jackson, she was called for an interview at the Baptist Hospital in Nashville. She got the job looking after kids with heart problems. They gave us three weeks to move. As big as that town was I knew I could find something too. I started in a plant making gas and electric stoves. The boys finished school. Robert got married and joined the Air Force. He was stationed in Maine and our first granddaughter was born up there.

Time passed. After ten years being a nurse she was getting a little burnt out. It was hard for her to see children die. We talked about it and as Nashville grew, the crime rate did too. So we thought it might be better if we moved to a smaller town. There wasn't much for us back in Jackson as my Dad had passed away in 1968. Her Mom died later, then three years later her Dad and some of her brothers and sisters passed away too. We decided to move to Calhoun, Georgia. Chris had joined the Knoxville Police Department and Curtis went to work in business in North Carolina then moved to Atlanta.

Jeanette was hired as a manager of the Dollar General store there and I went to work at Burlington Industries in nearby Shannon, changing later to Fafnir, a ball-bearing plant in Calhoun. She could have gone back into nursing but she'd just seen too much in Nashville. My shift ran from three in the afternoon till eleven. Everyday I'd go by the store an hour early to help Jeanette and Mrs. Roach put up stock. Later Mrs. Roach retired and they made

Jeanette the store manager. There was a young girl named Angie and GayeLynn that worked with her. They soon moved to a bigger, better store. She did such a good job there she got an award from Mr. Cal Turner for a million dollars of sales. In fact, I believe her store did the best in the state. The store grew so they had to hire three more. I think she got two or three hundred letters from customers saying how nice she'd treated them over the years.

In March of 1993, Calhoun was hit by a blizzard. Close to two feet of snow fell with driving winds. Power was knocked out everywhere. We woke up to a cold house and couldn't believe it when we looked outside. I cranked the van. We sat in it and warmed up. I asked her what she wanted to do. She wanted to go to the store. We made our way slowly down the driveway. Passing under the interstate, we saw traffic shut down both ways. Power lines and limbs were down. Roofs had caved in under so much snow. We got to the store and could easily see that the roof was in trouble. Her brother and I shoveled snow off that roof most of the next day. The store still had power though. Her brother stayed overnight with us at the store along with one of the girls who worked there and her children and another family who was without heat. Two men came by needing candles, blankets and food. They were stranded from Michigan. The Dollar General was about the only store open. When they got back they wrote a letter to the Calhoun newspaper saying how Jeanette was so nice to them. We wound up staying at the store for about a week.

I remember during that blizzard one of her workers had a son that died. I don't recall what happened but I remember walking in when Jeanette and Gracie were both crying. Jeanette closed the store the day of the funeral and gave Gracie a week off.

Another time when I stopped by Jeanette introduced me to a little eight-year-old boy. She called him her "little buddy". He couldn't walk. His parents had to tote him around. He had something wrong so he didn't grow right. There's a picture of Jeanette with him in her lap. She used to give him Matchbox cars. He couldn't talk either but those little cars always made him smile.

At Christmas, they had a special tree set up in the store. They called it the "Tree of Hope". Folks would come in and pick out a toy for a special little girl or boy who otherwise probably wasn't going to get anything for Christmas. Curtis and his wife often came down from Dahlonega and helped us decorate the store. Christmases were good back then. We had a big, four bedroom house. All the boys would come visit with their families.

Another Christmas, the plant I worked at was giving a Christmas party. The personnel lady knew Jeanette was the manager of the Dollar General. She asked if they would sell toys half-price for the kids.

After checking with her district manager Jeanette gladly said OK. After raising nearly $8000 at the plant, they came over to the store and Jeanette helped them pick out all kinds of toys. Jeanette and the two ladies from the plant wrapped all the presents and set everything up. She had that look on her face that she always had when she was helping others. She was so happy and I was so proud of her.

After being there ten years, she and I talked about doing something together to help poor people. They were talking about moving the store and Jeanette was thinking of opening her own place. I had retired at sixty-two, so I had time.

She'd been given a good bonus check by Cal Turner and had been saving it. She'd been saving it just for this. We leased a little building in the middle of town down by the high school. We worked days and nights cleaning and fixing it up except when we were in church. We had to put up clothes racks, shelving and a counter. We had a big stockroom. We spent over $3,000 fixing it up. We named it "The Grassroots Thrift and Donation Center". Our son Curtis came up with the name. Jeanette ran it for two months by herself then hired Melissa and Mrs. Ruby Laird.

We had donations coming in from everywhere. You name it, everything from clothes to furniture and appliances was coming in. Jeanette had two ladies helping her go through everything. The local Wal-Mart helped us with children's clothes and Kroger donated cakes, bread and buns for the needy. There was a family who'd lost everything in a fire we were able to help. There was a mother with two kids whose husband had left her that had rented a house but had no furniture at all. We took her three truckloads of furniture. Me, and one of the church members took it and we had our trucks loaded down. We took food to the church to help with their food pantry. In fact, half the food we got went to the church.

Jeanette fixed meals for the jail. She started helping the Pregnancy Center and the Battered Women's Shelter. It's not a pretty sight to see how some men beat on women and even their kids. Jeanette talked with the director there and they started having a Christmas party every year for those kids.

Jeanette loved to fish. Sometimes we'd get away and go to Carter's Lake or Lake Allatoona. Melissa would watch the store. We'd go see the grandkids every year. We'd go to Braves games back when they were in the old stadium. Jeanette liked football better. All our sons had played high school football. Her two favorite teams were the Dallas Cowboys and the Washington Redskins. Sometimes we'd go to a park and watch the deer. We had plenty to do around the house too. I had a peach orchard and an apple orchard, with several garden spots. We had a big yard. She'd get right in there with me, helping me mow or weed.

I remember one Sunday morning after we left church we stopped at the Dollar store to pick up a few things. She saw an old man sitting by a dumpster. He had slept in it the last two nights. We were on our way home so she told the man to wait and we'd be back with a meal. She sent me back with a meal, some ice tea, and a ten dollar bill. He wouldn't take the money. He thanked us and told me to tell Jeanette that God was looking down on her. We never saw him again.

There was a woman whose husband had run off with another woman. She had a daughter who wanted to go to college, but she knew she couldn't afford it. She came down to the store and asked Jeanette if she could help. Jeanette called a lady in administration at Dalton College and arranged an interview. Jeanette took them to see the lady and she gave the girl a grant and worked out a payment plan for the balance. The girl graduated three years later. She moved to North Carolina but sent us a picture and thanked Jeanette for what she'd done.

It wasn't just homefolks Jeanette was helping. She was helping the Indians in Oklahoma and New Mexico. She got together truckloads of food and clothes and W.H. Wright, who went to church with us and has a tractor-trailer, would haul it out there. When those Indians found out she died they sent me an award.

We first found out Jeanette had cancer in 1998. Dr. Howard had ordered X-rays but they came back clear. He wasn't satisfied and sent us to a specialist. Curtis' wife, Dori went with us. That doctor found it by physical examination. It was behind her right nipple, a spot that evidently X-rays didn't pick up. He ordered chemo to start the first of the next month. We had to go back and forth to Atlanta for the chemotherapy. It made her very sick and she lost her hair. Dori and I were with her each time. It was during one of those trips that she turned to me and said "Bob, we need to get in church and turn our lives over to God."

We got saved on Mother's Day and were both baptized. Later, the cancer went into remission for about eight or nine months, but it came back. We went to see Dr. Box there in Calhoun. It was in her right breast. She had to have her right breast removed or she would die. All of our sons came down to be with their mother. They removed it and several of her lymph nodes. They said they'd got it all and we were so happy.

Jeanette always got her mammograms every year. I can't stress how important it is for every woman out there to do this.

Her last Christmas party was in 2001. Cancer had come back on her. She was in a wheelchair. The disease was taking its toll on her. We'd fought it for years but she was in pretty bad shape and still was thinking of the kids. She cried when the last child left. I reckon she knew it would be her last Christmas party for those kids. I cried too.

I couldn't get her to stay home and rest, and the doctors couldn't either. She felt that working would keep her mind off of her health problems, and frankly, she didn't want to miss an opportunity to help somebody. That's the way she was.

The cancer worsened and she had to be hospitalized in 2002. She'd get better and come home and go back to work. As time passed it was found in her right lung as well. A new doctor got involved and started her off with chemo right away. The medicine he gave us was working well but after one month, he decided to switch it. We never did understand that. They did a biopsy of her right lung. Instead of taking a tissue sample, he removed half her lung. When the results came back, the doctor said there wasn't any cancer. Curtis was with me. I couldn't believe it. I couldn't believe what my wife of 48 years had been put through. I tried to ask the doctor more but he left the hospital.

In October 2002, she got worse and had to stay in until she came home in January of 2003. I stayed with her day and night. She was taking seventeen different medicines, but she was always as cheerful and sweet as she could be. We talked about the good old days and the rough times, too. We discussed how our boys had grown. Then we'd both wind up crying. We talked of how we first met and our early years together. She taught me that a good marriage has got to be fifty-fifty, and ours was. She also stressed the importance of living for God. I'm so proud of her and I miss her so.

Even near the end of her life she never quit trying to help others. One day I had to leave the hospital to run some errands. When I got back she wasn't in her hospital room. She'd had the nurse get her dressed and she was down in the children's wing. I found her there reading to the kids about Jesus. When we left the hospital the kids gave her a big card. They'd all signed it.

Curtis moved back to Tennessee in January of 2003. He invited us to come live with him for a while. We stayed with them a couple of weeks. The nurse had told me that Jeanette might last one more week. I stayed up sitting beside her and finally laid down. Curtis came and got me. I held Jeanette knowing she was with God and the angels.

Jeanette died January 26, 2003. She was buried three days later. There were almost four hundred people there. It was cold and drizzling rain. As I looked at my three sons, Robert, Curtis and Chris, I knew she was with God. Curtis spoke at her funeral.

This is a portion of what he said, how he described his mother:

"...She lived for us and she lived because of us. Today and forever, we'll miss her...Mother was the one who waved goodbye to us and the one who welcomed us home. My memories of her are homemade teacakes and popcorn in an iron skillet saturated in Crisco and covered in real butter and salt...She had breast cancer, lung cancer and bone cancer but on December 23rd a year ago in a wheelchair and on oxygen she gave Christmas toys and groceries to thirty-five needy families..."

I was blessed to have her for my wife for 48 years. She was a sweet and loving mother to our sons. We learned a lot from her. She was always putting us first, never herself. She came off a run-down farm in Tennessee, not having anything much, except for love for her family and fellow man. She was a strong, Christian woman and I feel like she's looking down on us and watching over us today. Someday we'll meet her again on God's golden shore. We miss you "Mama", but you'll always be in our hearts and souls.

I'd go to her grave four or five times a day, everyday.

Robert, our first-born, and his wife Kathy have given us three grandchildren: Amanda, Misty, and Robert. After a serving in the Air Force, Robert and Kathy came back to Tennessee where he now works with the state patrol. Their son, Robert, is a Marine. He's been to Iraq twice and has two kids. Amanda and Misty are married too, with two kids each.

Curtis went to college in Knoxville then worked in Arkansas, North Carolina and Georgia. He helped Jeanette and me fix up the thrift store on the weekends. He helped her at the Battered Women's shelter too. He really got a kick at Christmas helping her shop for two to three hundred kids. He got married to Dori, in 1999, and has two kids, Cooper and Kinsley.

Chris went into law enforcement in Chattanooga in the Drug Task Force and later teamed up in the canine squad. He married Rhonda and they have a little girl. He moved on up and made chief of police. Later having being diagnosed as a diabetic, he quit the force.

Jeanette and I were blessed with three good, loving sons. We were blessed with each other. We were blessed with learning the value of hard work and hard times, to be grateful for the little things and most of all to fear and trust God. I'd seen something in Jeanette's eyes a long time ago. I saw a glitter of hope in her to help people no matter how young or old. If they needed food, clothing, furniture or a place to stay, she did what she could. I remember one lady came in with a sick child. She didn't have enough money to buy the child's medicine. Jeanette gave her the money.

On July 26, 2004, the mayor of Calhoun, Georgia signed a resolution honoring Jeanette for her unselfish and tireless service at the Grass Roots Thrift Shop, the Voluntary Action Center, the Pregnancy Center and the United Way Helpline. There's also a plaque from the St. Joseph's Indian School thanking Jeanette for her support of the Lakota people. The editor of the Calhoun Times wrote an article about how Jeanette had helped the community.

I'd also like to thank all the good people of Calhoun especially Sid Roberts, Dr. Box, Dr. Howard, Willie Mitchell, Judge Broyles, Cathy Harrison, Jimmy Palmer the mayor, and Judge Fuller for being so nice to Jeanette. I want to add also how much I appreciate our pastor, Keith Reed and his son Tim. They were with us many times. I want to thank Mr. W.H. Wright for getting those trucks to haul supplies to the Indian reservations and also for always playing Santa Claus at the Christmases for the kids. Thank you Melissa and your husband Johnny. You were always right in there with us and were great friends.

> "Do not let your hearts be troubled. Trust in God, trust also in me. In my Father's house are many rooms; if it were not so, I would have told you. I am going there to prepare a place for you. And if I go and prepare a place for you, I will come back and take you to be with me that you also may be where I am. You know the way to the place where I am going." John 14:1-4

The Army issued me a little Bible. I carried it in Korea in my pocket over my heart. I must have read Psalms 23 hundreds of times: "The Lord is my shepherd; I shall not be in want. He makes me lie down in green pastures, he leads me beside quiet waters, he restores my soul. He guides me in paths of righteousness for his name's sake. Even though I walk through the valley of the shadow of death, I will fear no evil, for you are with me; your rod and your staff, they comfort me. You prepare a table before me in the presence of mine enemies. You anoint my head with oil; my cup overflows. Surely goodness and love will follow me all the days of my life, and I will dwell in the house of the Lord forever." Psalm 23

I guess Eugene helped me more than he ever knew. If you ever go to the new park in downtown Calhoun, Georgia, as you're walking, look down. There are three bricks with her name on them in memory of her.

Annie

Annie

For a year after she died I slept on top of the bedcovers. Without her it just didn't make sense anymore. Why bother unwrapping the present if there's nothing inside? I didn't see any reason to turn down the sheets anymore. Everything I wanted in a wife and in a marriage she gave me.

She walked into my office in March of 1999. I was the plant manager of a north Georgia textile mill. We needed a tufting machine operator, which is a skilled labor position on equipment that made pattern rugs. Through an inside source we heard about two women that were working somewhere

My Girl

else that might be interested. So after talking with the supervisor I decided to ask them in for an interview. Only needing one, I figured we'd just hire the first one or the better of the two. No big deal.

Something about her struck me the second I saw her. She was friendly, pretty, confident and a little shy. What grabbed me was; it was clear she could take it or leave it.

Nothing she said or did conveyed this, but somehow I knew this strong, intelligent girl would be just fine whether or not she got the job. Being a fairly down-to-earth guy I'm not much for pretense but I was used to a little deference. She didn't give me any.

After the interview I told her we'd let her know and she gave me a polite smile and walked out. I had no idea if she was married or not. We didn't ask that. All I knew was something inside me clicked and I sat down after she'd left feeling like I'd just been

My Girl

hit by a hammer. We sent word the next day that she had the job. It was brought back to me that she'd only take the job if I'd hire her friend, Tammy too. Well that was a fine box of chocolates! I talked with Ed, the supervisor, and CJ the master mechanic, and persuaded them we could try two operators. For a privately owned mill in a small southern town we had plenty of women on the job but not on a big machine. Things were about to change, for me, and the plant.

Soon Annie and Tammy broke the gender barrier in our little world and that was that. Being divorced less than a year at the time I was very cautious around attractive girls and from a professional standpoint as well. As weeks passed I could hear the laughter from the breakroom as Tammy, the more mischievous of the two, tried to stay ahead of CJ whose sense of humor was legendary. But it was Annie's laugh that seemed to stand out. Intentionally avoiding contact, by circumstance we'd pass each other and sometimes we'd speak, sometimes I'd just nod and move on. She seemed to me to be a mystery that I needed to solve, a pull that I couldn't define.

I'd been praying for God to give me a good girl, the right girl. Unlike my younger years I didn't see my single status as the buffet. I really had no interest in dating. If only He'd bring me the right girl. As more weeks passed I routinely walked the line of machines as I had before, but now I wasn't trying to walk around her as I had been. I walked past her and we spoke. Then that smile, those green eyes and that captivating laugh grabbed me like some romantic tracking beam. This naturally scared me to death.

I remember going home and praying, asking God to give me a girl like her. Someone sweet and easy-going, as pleasant as a summer breeze, that's who I needed, someone just like her. The next Monday morning she asked if I'd had a good weekend; if I'd gone out on a date…etc. I replied negatively, trying not to burst into flames. She smiled and laughed her little laugh. Like a junebug flying right for a bug zapper that was it for me. I knew it and I was coming in hot. Still having no idea if she was married, I was terrified to look at her left hand, knowing I'd be crushed if she was married. As weeks turned to months, the attraction became obvious as the more forward of our co-workers, mostly C.J. and Tammy, tried to bring each to the other's attention.

Then one day it happened. She asked me if I was dating anyone. I gulped, answered "No" then asked about her. She replied that she was unhappily married.

Believe me nobody was more unhappy, to hear that she was married, than me. Looking into those sparkling green eyes, seeing her vulnerability, knowing I was falling in love with her, I said, "I'm looking for a girl, the right girl, but I want a marriage that's right with God. You need to go back to your husband, tell him whatever it is he needs to do and try to save your marriage. If it doesn't work out and you file for divorce, then we'll go out..." The words were out of my mouth before I had a chance to reconsider. Watching her walk away, sensing inside me that she was the one, was worse than being kicked in the stomach and dragged through fire ants.

Time passed and we were tentatively friendly. Then she told me she'd tried and she was going to file for divorce. She asked if I'd meet her after work to talk. We met and we talked. Being with her that afternoon, just talking, was simply the most beautiful, exciting time I've ever had. We talked like old friends, discussing anything and everything. We held hands. I put my arm around her and finally we kissed. Like a drink of cool spring water we couldn't get enough. We kissed and hugged and cried and laughed and kissed some more. The passion between us raging like a three alarm fire, we knew we'd have to stop or we wouldn't be able to. We did stop and we prayed together. We asked for God to forgive us for jumping the gun a little, but now that the die was cast to please protect her and if it was His will to make everything go smoothly to formally end her marriage and bless us, have His hand on us and have His will for us.

She'd been going to night school to get her GED. Here was this hard-scrabble country girl who'd quit school in the sixth grade, working in a hot mill ten hours a day then going to night school. She was chosen to give a speech at the commencement. She invited me. When she got up on stage my heart swelled. I knew she was nervous but she did fine. Her plain-spoken genuineness and sweetness radiated from her. Afterwards as we mingled at the reception she introduced me as her "fiancee'" to some of her friends.

My Girl

She was a little ahead of me on that one and it hit me like a lightning bolt, but I quickly decided more in my heart than in my head, she just may be right.

We started dating. We tried to keep things strictly professional at work, and I told my boss, who was reservedly happy for me. We did keep things proper at work but the attraction between us was tangible and so unreservedly total. We were like two little kids who were such good friends they start giggling when they meet. You couldn't put 100 eight-year olds in the middle of Santa's workshop and match the giddiness that Annie and I felt when we were together.

She kept going to night school, this time to community college, to get a respiratory therapist degree. I'd go by on my way home and leave flowers or notes on her car. If it wasn't too late she'd come out to my house and we'd spend a precious hour or two together. I swear kissing her goodbye and watching her drive away just killed me. I can still see her beaming face. The night air was magical. I'd kiss her and then chase her car down and kiss her some more. She never could outrun me.

Then I'd go inside and wait forty-five minutes for her to call to say she was home safe. I was 42 and felt sixteen again.

I remember one clear, star-filled night I was walking her out to her car praying silently, asking God if she was the one. I sure believed it, but I didn't want to hurt her and I didn't want to be squashed again either. I was ready to slide the whole pile over; all chips in. As soon as we stepped outside a falling star swept slowly across the night sky. It looked like God was holding a huge sparkler and just waved it at us. We both felt it and again I prayed silently, "She's the one, isn't she Father?" This time another shooting star, much faster, streaked across the sky. We kissed under the stars and I watched her drive away. I was all in.

I'd bring her gardenia flowers that grow by my pool when I saw her in the mornings. She gave me notes and I wrote her poetry. I'd help her with her homework at night. As those sweet, soft summer nights passed something happened that changed everything.

As my son, William and I helped my brother Eddie, move into his new house on a sweltering Saturday that Labor Day weekend, something hit me. I felt as if I'd been punched in the stomach, doubling me over. Later that day we found out that our brother, Neal, had died of a sudden arrhythmia that morning while he was hiking with his middle daughter. Here was a good, hard-working husband and father of three little girls suddenly dead at 39.

As Annie and I fell deeper in love, I knew that I didn't want to, that I couldn't, waste any more time. I talked to my wonderful kids, Christine, who was seventeen and William, who was twelve and told them I was going to ask Annie to marry me. They were protective of me, cognizant of the fact that my marriage to their mother had been such a fabulous disaster, but knew Annie and I loved each other and she made me happy.

A few weeks later I asked her to spend the weekend with me. When I picked her up she gave me a dozen roses and I had a dozen for her too. Nobody had ever given me flowers before and I was thrown off a little but Annie just grinned. We stayed at the Woodbridge Inn, a bed and breakfast inn in Jasper, Georgia, with a really good restaurant. I reserved the table by the aquarium and after dinner I got down on one knee and proposed.

She accepted and we planned a small Christmas Eve wedding at our church, Victory Temple Church of God in Calhoun. I've always been a sucker for Christmas, for spiritual, sentimental, and traditional reasons. The way I saw it, God was giving me the best Christmas present ever. We had a small wedding, simple and sweet. My older brother, Ken was my best man and Annie's Dad gave her away. Annie's daughter, Marie, was the maid of honor and her two little girls Hallie and Destiny were flower girls. Her son Matt was there too. Annie's son Derek and my son William were groomsmen and my sweet daughter Christine was there. My parents had already passed away as had Annie's mother but the rest of our families were there.

We spent that night, Christmas Eve, together at my house sharing a bottle of champagne by the fire as the Christmas tree twinkled behind us. We spent Christmas with our kids then left for our honeymoon at Forrest Hills near Dahlonega, Georgia. We stayed at the "love nest" cabin. It was a rustic cabin with a four-post canopy bed, den with a fireplace, nice little kitchen and the proverbial hot tub in the bedroom. We spent our days horseback riding, hiking, sight-seeing, talking, laughing and being together. We spent our nights praying together thanking God for the beautiful blessing He'd given us.

She was my "Cinderella" and I was her "Romeo" and to tell Annie's story, she was a Cinderella girl. Believe me nobody belonged at the ball more than her. She just didn't know it. She had humble beginnings but worked tenaciously to better herself before and during our marriage, right up until she died. A girl or anyone with a sweeter spirit I've never met. I recall a story she'd written for homework. She told about how most Christmases when she was a child she didn't get any presents. The only Santa Claus she ever knew was a blonde lady stranger who left gifts and food on their porch one year and drove away. Not having any toys she simply went out into the woods and made a playhouse under a fallen tree using a pine branch to sweep the dirt floor. My family wasn't rich by any means. We were solidly middle class but I don't have a clue much less a concept of what life was like for her. Sure "things" don't make Life but I never experienced Life with virtually no "things". Maybe that's why she pushed herself. Maybe that's why she appreciated anything and everything.

We came home and settled in. We lived at my house with Christine and William. Her son, Derek, having shown a rebellious nature, was going to keep her place, a nice, clean trailer with a built-on front deck on four acres, and live there, with it becoming his in the future. Annie's fine daughter Marie was already married to Mickey, a good, hard-working young man and they lived in town.

We returned to the plant, this time as husband and wife. One of the mill girls had married one of the bosses. That was true, but I don't see things that way. We're all in the same race and it's a marathon. Sure some are given a head start, some start way in the back but this "better than you" stuff is a load of horse-puckey. Let's see what you do with what you've got. Annie was the embodiment of that. We'd put in a new software system to run our business and I asked Annie if she'd like to learn how to enter production on a computer. It scared her because she'd never really worked on one and she was a little self-conscious about her lack of formal education, but she did, and did fine. She continued going to night school and worked hard. At the point where she would begin taking actual medically-related courses, her school was brought under the control of another college and the privileged geniuses there saw fit to not count all the English, math and literature she and everyone else in a medical program had already been credited with. In effect she'd gone to night school to get her GED and then another year of community college and that last year was down the drain. Those geniuses should have been horse-whipped.

Broken-hearted but not broken, she decided to change schools. She didn't trust that bunch anymore and I didn't blame her. She started at Dalton State about twenty minutes up the interstate from work. She was doing fine until she ran into an English teacher who failed papers for something as subjective as a misplaced comma. If only teachers would teach! She couldn't get past that. She heard about dialysis training. We talked and prayed about it. Here was my wife, a very smart girl who'd busted her butt at farm work, cleaning houses, and mill-work all her life. I wanted to see her in better working conditions. She decided to go for it. She did great. She quit her job at the plant and starting working as a dialysis technician in Cartersville. Soon her friend Tammy joined her.

They do routine blood tests in those jobs and that Christmas Eve on our first anniversary we found out Annie had been infected with Hepatitis C. She'd been in a brutal car crash twenty years before. Her first husband, Robert, Marie's Dad, had died beside her. Annie's back was broken. Her left arm was broken. They'd had to put steel pins in both. She had the scars to prove it.

She'd had to stay in a body-cast for a year and on that terrible night, she got some bad blood. She recalled being jaundiced but the medical community knew Hepatitis-C only as non-A, non-B then, and she was told not to worry about it. Fast forward twenty years and here's a sweet strong girl finally moving ahead only to find out that it did matter and it's a slow killer, and now she's scared to death her new husband's going to tell her to hit the road.

She told me and it broke my heart but only for a moment. It was clear she didn't know she had it. She'd told me about the accident before. What was even clearer was I loved this girl. I knew God had put us together. It scared me but I thought we'd learn

My Girl

as much as we could and fight this thing and beat it together. I held her and kissed her and we prayed. I told her there was no way I was going to let her down. I loved her and whatever we faced, high or low, we faced it together. So we moved ahead. We changed her diet and stopped drinking our weekend bottle of wine.

There were more star-filled nights and nights cuddling on the front porch in the hammock looking at the moon. There were hectic weekdays, birthdays and events for my kids and hers and her grandchildren. There were romantic dinners out and romantic dinners in. Alone, sometimes we'd sneak and skinny-dip in the pool but the best times were Sundays for me. When we'd go to church together I'd feel like my life was in total balance. At peace and in harmony with God, with a spirit-filled wife that wasn't uncomfortable when the preachin' got a little loud and the congregation shouted. She was from a country background and that didn't bother her a lick. In fact, we felt that God's presence should shake things up. Most city people would be looking for the exits, but I don't believe that way and neither did she. When God moves people, people are moved, and it's hard to sit there with your hands folded checking your watch. Being in church with her, our spirits in tune with each other and with God was almost indescribably wonderful. After church we'd usually spend a lazy afternoon together watching a movie, and then enjoying a long nap. Sunday was our special day. It was the closest to Heaven I've ever been.

I truly believe that women in their forties are at their most beautiful. Still retaining a blush of their youth, the trials they've survived and the character they build show on their faces too. A woman in her forties just presents more strength and wisdom than younger girls do. That is incredibly sexy. We celebrated her 40th birthday the following February. The

My Girl

only wrinkles she had were laugh lines. She still had a body like a cheerleader and a face like a model...but the quiet strength, determination, perseverance, and her sweet spirit made her stunning. Not a day went by that I didn't thank God for her and that we didn't say "I love you", most days many times. We were both so incredibly grateful for each other. I look back on those days, still years before the disease would begin exacting such a heavy price, and they were too fleeting and so very precious.

Annie's workdays started early. Her alarm went off at 4:30 since she had to be in Cartersville by six. She'd usually work four ten-hour days. She'd told me of a recurring dream she'd had before she started working there. She would see herself walking beside older people covered by sheets and that's what she wound up doing.

Working in dialysis can be tough emotionally, as patients that you grow fond of, worsen and sometimes die. The job is filtering blood, so workplace accidents can be a little unnerving too. Annie would come home and tell me about her day and she just had a way about her. Sometimes she'd be deeply troubled over a patient's condition or maybe they'd be short-handed and she was just bone-tired. But Annie would always be Annie. We'd hug and I'd hold her. Then I'd gaze into those serene green eyes and pull her closer and she'd smile that beautiful, peaceful smile. Somehow, it radiated from her that she had an incredible trust and faith in God and love for me. It just beamed from her.

She had a lot of friends that she worked with and her patients loved her, because she loved them. Sure some of them were old cranks, but Annie could hang in there with them and her sweetness would eventually melt them. There was one time that the clinic threw a Christmas party. I couldn't go. My darling wife, against all convention, broke loose and got thoroughly snockered. I remember getting a phone call and Becky, a co-worker, had to drive her home. I helped her inside amidst her apologies and put her gently to bed. I remember kissing her hair and crying and smiling at the same time. I knew it was bad for her to drink but she had an awful lot of pressure on her. I guess she wanted to be "normal" that night and kick up her heels a little. The next day Annie was completely ashamed and apologetic. Sometimes you have to bust loose a little I guess.

She had a little white Pontiac. It was time to trade it in so we went car shopping. She was being practical, looking at four-door sedans mostly, when I saw two like-new convertibles. One was white with a black top and gray leather interior and the other one was dark gray. I steered her over towards them and she gave me that little sideways "Are you serious look?". They both had low miles and still under warranty. I grinned and hugged her. We drove them and she picked the white one. She'd never had a convertible before. She was so happy she started crying. She loved riding in that car with Marie and her girls.

Annie never had to have anything expensive. She had simple wants. A walk down to the creek in the back, or lying in the hammock looking at the stars suited her just fine. When I did get her something nice, she just melted. Thing was, she appreciated everything.

Annie worked a second job occasionally in home health care. She had one patient that she just loved. She was pretty much bed-ridden and barely weighed ninety pounds. I'm not sure how old she was, I'd guess in her thirties. Her home didn't have air conditioning. Georgia summers can be stifling. Annie bought an air conditioner for her and we went over and put it in. She was crazy about Annie too.

The months and years passed and our sweet life together continued. We started seeing specialists for her liver. She got a biopsy done. It showed mild cirrhosis but it wasn't too bad. She tried the latest drug therapy. It was an anti-viral drug and an interferon treatment. She gave herself the shots as long as she could until she had to come off of it since her blood counts were plummeting. That left us only one medical option, a liver transplant.

We prayed together every night and I'd hold her reassuring her everything was going to turn out fine. She was still working but it seemed like she'd tire more easily. She was sleeping a little more and she started losing muscle mass. Our first real scare came when she was diagnosed with gall bladder problems during the spring of 2003. It was bad and was going to have to come out. It was going to be done laparoscopically and was a really routine procedure.

The operation went fine and Annie did great. The scare came when they took a picture of her liver. I asked to see it. I never told her what I saw. Her liver was markedly worse than the biopsy photo taken just a few years before. I knew we were up against something serious but that photo slapped me pretty hard. All I could do was just try to be everything she needed even harder, and of course I prayed harder. The second thing that happened was that she was given saline solution in her IV. For a liver patient on diuretics, that didn't make much sense. We got to learn what ascites was as her tummy swelled so big it looked like she'd swallowed a basketball. It scared us both but they got it under control and we came home.

Annie recuperated quickly and returned to work. There's an old saying that someone with a lot of courage and drive had "grit". Annie had it by the truckload.

In the fall of 2003 we traveled to Birmingham to the UAB hospital. She was tested thoroughly, physically and mentally. Her heart, lungs and everything were fine, everything but her liver. The staff and doctors were very nice. We treated it like a romantic getaway and actually had a good time. Her MELD score, which is a composite of three attributes relating to liver function, was still too good to be placed on the transplant list, which was fine with us. We were accepted into the program and were told to keep getting checked and scheduled to return in the future.

We also changed from a local specialist to a doctor in Atlanta. This guy was incredible. He was a kind, older doctor who spoke with an English accent. He was amazingly thorough and one of the most intelligent men I've ever met. He checked Annie methodically, calling out a list of symptoms to his able, young assistant. Her spleen was slightly enlarged and she had "spider-veins" on her skin. He seemed to know everything about Annie's condition before we said anything. He seemed to warm to Annie who had a disarming charm and she liked him, too, which was even better.

We saw him about once a month. Due to the liver's function of filtering fluid, she had to start taking medicine to regulate fluid in her body since her liver was impaired. We were also told to watch her diet, especially for ammonia, since the liver filtered it out of the blood and if it was high it would cause confusion and even worse. We watched her diet even closer and she took her medicine on schedule. I know she was trying to do her best and I think she was trying to show the Doc what a good girl she'd been too.

We treated the trips to Atlanta like a fun event for us since we were together. We had a change in insurance, which didn't cover UAB anymore and had to get in the Emory transplant program. Her doctor got that initiated and soon we traveled to Emory for their battery of tests. Like Birmingham, they tested everything and like Birmingham everything was fine except for her liver, which had worsened. Unlike Birmingham, they tried to transplant patients with the higher (worse) MELD scores. UAB tried to prioritize transplants with a higher degree of patient success in mind so if a patient with a lower MELD score was healthy otherwise they may get transplanted ahead of someone who was in worse shape but their survivability may have been marginal. At least that's the way I understood it, and at that time Annie's scores were still relatively low so it was a disappointment because it seemed she may have gotten a quicker transplant at UAB.

We started seeing the Emory Transplant Clinic doctors. As Annie's liver declined and her MELD score rose she was officially listed. We also soon saw how whatever marginal tolerances her body had were getting slimmer and slimmer. She started getting fatigued much faster and they started having to build up her blood. We were going routinely once a month, then every other week, then weekly.

She was still working, but barely. To work one day she'd have to rest one or maybe two. She'd just finished going to a technical school earning a phlebotomy certification. Even sick, the girl kept reaching for something better.

We started seeing the first signs of ammonia buildup as at times we made dietary mistakes and she would become disoriented. She was scared and we talked and we prayed. One night her fluid built up alarmingly in her belly. We were afraid, but determined we'd go to the hospital in the morning if we had to. We prayed that night and I held her as she cried softly. We felt God's presence and after touching each other and more prayer and talking we fell asleep. In the morning I kissed her and reluctantly drew back the covers to check her tummy. It was perfectly flat. Normal. She looked down amazed and I stared in wonder, praising God. (She hadn't gotten up during the night at all. Her belly had gone from a pumpkin to a pancake.) Elated, we kissed and hugged, certain that the Lord was with us. I squeezed her again. We prayed together and thanked Him.

I remember walking out into the plant still shaken by what I'd seen, fearfully asking Him if He'd healed her. He told me "I don't do things halfway…." Later at work I saw Mickey, a good friend of mine. He and his wife, Alice go to our church and usually sat next to Annie and me. I told him what had happened. We both felt it was a miracle and in my office we prayed for Annie and thanked God.

I'll go to my grave knowing that God made her belly flat that morning and that He spoke to me also. At the time I saw it as I wanted to and as I needed to, that either He had healed her or if He hadn't totally healed her He was going to.

As a few more weeks passed and we got into the summer of 2004 it seemed any tolerance or margin we enjoyed with her liver function evaporated and all the complications associated with end-stage liver disease cascaded down onto us. The ascites started becoming more often but now the fluid was backing up into her chest cavity compressing her right lung. The dysphoria connected to elevated ammonia became more frequent. We started what would become a grueling gauntlet of ambulance rides, hospital stays, procedures, operations and nights fearing they were her last.

They started having to draw out 2 liters of fluid from her right lung cavity. It would come back the next day. Since her liver wasn't filtering fluid normally it just built up. It got so bad that we went to a hospital closer to home in Rome. The doctors there felt the thing to do was to somehow seal the space between the chest wall and the lung so the fluid couldn't back up in there. I tried to talk to our specialist in Atlanta but couldn't get him and after asserting that these doctors should talk to him we agreed to do it. That was one of the big things I learned. Doctors don't always share information, even in the same hospital, even when they're supposed to, even when they're asked to.

The operation didn't work. The chest cavity needed to be dry for it to and it wasn't going to happen the way Annie's liver was. The old doctor's dismay was evident when I finally spoke to him. So the procedure done to alleviate the symptoms wasn't effective because the root cause had become so pronounced. Annie spent a month with a chest tube in. We were then told that she needed a "TIPS" procedure, sort of a liver bypass to divert some of the blood going to the liver to reduce the fluid amount it would have to filter.

The old Doc endorsed it so we transferred back to Emory to have it done. We'd already had some nightmares with her ammonia levels requiring ambulance rides and hospital stays so the concept of intentionally putting more unfiltered blood to her brain was not appealing. You want Door #1 or Door #2? You want to drown internally or die from ammonia poisoning? I'd already had a well-intentioned chaplain tell me it was time to say goodbye during one of our emergencies.

There was one particular time that her ammonia was high. They couldn't get it down despite the things they do. Despite my faith and what we had already been through and what we were going through; that night was so terrible, it overwhelmed me. It was about five or six that morning. We'd gotten into the ER around seven the night before. Marie and her husband Mickey had come down too and they had gone home after staying the whole night. I was in the room with my wife, the woman I loved, my Annie. She was restrained because she was in such bad shape. It was awful and that's an understatement. She'd be sound asleep for, at most, five minutes or so, then she'd be wide awake and stare wildly, pulling at the straps, then she'd fall back asleep. It went on all night.

Her body chemistry was so messed up because the ammonia was so high. To see someone go through hell is one thing. To see someone you love, your mate and partner, your best friend, go through hell is something else. It gripped me and it swallowed me. It wasn't the first time we'd been on this horse, but usually it would be over by morning.

I started crying and I couldn't stop. I was shaking and sobbing like a baby. A nurse came in and saw me. I guess she's used to a lot. I imagine she'd seen a lot. She spoke to me and looked at me. I think I scared her a little. I didn't mean to but I cried like that for almost an hour and now it was being planned to put more unfiltered blood to Annie. I'd stop crying and start again. I knew that God was real and that He was in control but He felt so very far away. I just didn't feel like her dying was a possibility even though my sweet girl and I'd been walking through that valley for a long time already.

The TIPS went well and after a while they were able to finally remove the chest tube. It stopped the fluid buildup. The old Doc was right. She recovered. She had to formally go on leave from her job, which she hated. Annie felt like she wasn't pulling her weight, which was a foreign reality for her. So at home she'd do more than she should and get tired much quicker than either one of us was used to.

The symptoms kept snowballing on us. If her ammonia wasn't high her red blood counts were low. We were going to the clinic weekly. Soon she was getting blood almost every time we went to the clinic to be checked. About every other time Annie was in such bad shape we'd have to be admitted. It got to be a roll of the dice every time we went down whether we'd stay or not.

I'd been wearing a beeper in case a liver came available. In August it went off. I called the clinic and they confirmed that they wanted us to come down. Annie was nervous but she was more excited about being better than she was scared. The faith that she showed still amazes me. Even in our quiet times when sometimes she would cry and we'd speak softly to each other and I would hold her; she knew she was in God's hands.

We called her daughter, Marie and told my kids and everyone else. Soon we were up on the transplant floor and the nurses were getting Annie prepped for surgery. We saw the choppers take off and land outside. We prayed that Annie would be OK. After several hours a dejected doctor came into the room.

He told us the organ was bad and couldn't be used. We were disappointed but felt that the Lord was taking care of us by avoiding a bad organ and of course we prayed for the donor's family.

We went back home, down, but kept our chins up. Annie had told the church that if God would just let her feel good enough to come back to church she wanted to sing a special song. The lines of the song are, "Yes, Lord, yes to Your will and to Your way. Yes, Lord, yes I will trust You and obey." He did. He gave us a miracle month when she didn't have to be admitted and she was in pretty good shape. That Sunday she sang for the whole church. For a shy girl it was a big step. For a wonderful girl trusting in the Lord it seemed real natural. Everybody knew what a battle she was in. The pastor and several members had been out to the house praying for her often. She was now just a shell of her former physical self but that Sunday she shined like the stars in heaven and the angels were in the choir loft. Annie was radiant. She sang and I've never been prouder of her courage and her sweet spirit.

We reveled in that delicious respite. God gave us a break and I thank Him. That sweet interlude, all too brief, ended.

Her condition worsened and the disease came back with a vengeance. We were back to staying in the hospital more days than we were home. One night at home I woke up to Annie crying softly. She asked, "Honey, did you see them?" Scanning the clock which was somewhere around 3AM, I slid my arms around her and replied, "No, baby…" She sighed and said, "Oh honey, it was beautiful. The angels…they were everywhere. It was so beautiful…" She was never scared again.

It seems like we were stuck in a revolving door in and out of the hospital. The biggest problem we were having was Annie's low blood counts. It had been bad blood that had given her this and we were about to get dealt another bad hand. We were back in. It was late October. My son William's football team was doing great. It was Friday night and one of their playoff games. Annie's blood was so low when we went for our doctor's visit they'd admitted us and ordered four bags of blood for her.

It was late when the third bag started. She began vomiting. Her heart rate and blood pressure started going crazy. The nurses seemed stunned. I held a basin and tried to clean Annie up. The nurses rechecked the blood type and verified it was correct. I pointed out Annie's heart rate, which would jump and fall, then jump again. I asked if they should stop the blood but they left the room and returned with some monitoring equipment. This time they did stop the blood and took that bag off. They put the other bag on and Annie stabilized.

They ordered an echocardiogram the following Monday. It was abnormal. They didn't tell me, or her transplant physicians, who work in the same hospital. I have a hard time understanding that. We went home. I got a blood pressure machine to check her with at home. The next week we went back to the doctor and they had to keep her again. Her transplant doctor was getting very concerned about Annie's overall condition and they kept us again.

That Wednesday Annie was in good enough shape to go home. We'd almost made it back when the beeper went off. She started praising God and was so happy. We turned back. Again they got Annie ready for surgery. They had a hard time getting an IV started. The nurse kept wanting to "try". Finally I insisted she get someone else. They did and she got a vein. Annie's heart rate started fluctuating wildly. They gave her some medicine to control it but it would only help temporarily. By now it was late, two or three in the morning. The cardiologist on call came by and nothing they did kept her heart rate from jumping. The nurses started getting real worried.

They took her back and we kissed and I prayed. It was almost dawn now. A guy from the transplant team came in the waiting room. By the look on his face I knew it was bad. He told me that because of Annie's heart rate they couldn't give her the organ and transplanted another patient. It felt like everything inside me just got broken. I felt so bad for my girl. When I saw her I could tell how hurt she was. We talked and I kissed her and we prayed together.

In the following days more cardiologists came to see her. They gave her some medicine that seemed to regulate her heart and as each day passed my sweet Annie faded. She declined so they had to put us in ICU. It wasn't our first time but we knew we were up against a wall now. Her transplant surgeon came to see me that Saturday. He was baffled by Annie's heart problems and asked me if I was aware of anything that had happened. I looked at him incredulously and told him about the transfusion reaction about two weeks before, naively thinking he was aware of it. He seemed very troubled and said he'd order an echocardiogram on Monday to check for heart damage. I told him that they'd done one the Monday after that had happened but I'd never heard anything about it. I looked at him unbelievingly, shocked that he wasn't aware of what had happened. He told me he was going to go find it and see what it said.

When he returned later I knew it was bad. He'd found it and it showed her heart was damaged. He was angry. He told me he was ordering another for that Monday. He looked me in the eye and told me that if Annie's heart had a chance, he'd transplant her as fast as he could, but if it was too badly damaged, he couldn't. I understood and I appreciate him being so open with me. I still can't swallow that the other personnel hadn't informed the transplant team of what had happened.

So, I knew that on Monday we'd know what doctors could or couldn't do for us. Annie was, by now, sleeping most of the time. She had a male nurse who was a really attentive and good guy. He knew she was in really bad shape. When she was awake I told her what was going on, but not to worry that God would see us through. She looked at me with so much love in her eyes and I sensed that she knew so much more than I did.

I came home to check on the kids and go to work the next morning. Marie stayed with Annie. My son, William went hunting in the back with my brother, Eddie, and he killed his first buck. Life goes on.

That night I called a few close friends and talked to Christine and William and prayed harder than I ever have. I knew she was in God's hands. I asked him to totally heal her, heart, liver and all...or just touch her heart so she could get transplanted. I mean it wasn't fair that bad blood had given her that damn disease and bad blood was going to slap her down again.

I went to work the next day feeling fairly confident that in His way He'd work it out. I left and drove back to the hospital. I wasn't there long before the nurse coordinator walked heavily towards me. She started crying before she could tell me that the test showed significant heart damage and that there wasn't anything they could do. She said that Annie may just have a day or two, a week at most. They could keep her in the hospital where they'd keep her sedated or if I wanted, I could take her home. I talked to Marie and told her I was bringing her mother home. After I called everybody I sucked it down and walked in to see Annie. She was sleeping but woke when I touched her hand. I told her what the doctors said. She looked at me with such serenity and told me it was OK and that everything would be all right. She asked if I'd take her home and I told her, "Yeah, I'm takin' you home baby." We kissed and she drifted back to sleep.

We came home. They brought a hospital bed out and the Hospice nurses came. At night I'd lay down next to her and talk to her and kiss her and hold her. She wasn't talking much anymore and sleeping most of the time. Marie told Annie's Dad, nieces and nephews, sisters and brothers and they all came out that Friday to see her and talk to her. Of course Marie had Mickey and her children and Christine and William were with me. Late in the day Annie's son showed up. Tammy and some of Annie's coworkers were there.

That night after everyone had gone, I laid down with her again and about two I whispered in her ear, "Kiss me baby…" and she leaned up and kissed me.

My Girl

The next morning I touched her and she was cold. I took her in my arms and begged God to breathe LIFE back into her. He didn't. I bathed her and kissed her from head to toe and told her how much I loved her and how proud I was of her. I thanked her for being my wife and for being such a good one.

At her funeral, Richard from where she worked, sang "I'll Fly Away". It was one of her favorite songs. In the same church where we were married less than five years before, a beautiful young woman lay surrounded by friends, music, flowers and family. But Life is like that. There's a time to laugh and a time to cry. I just thank Him again for the time that He gave me with Annie.

About a month after she died I wrote this letter. It was published in our local paper:

Tribute to a Good Wife

The Bible says that a good wife is worth far more than rubies. (see Proverbs 31: 10-31) I humbly assert that's an understatement. My sweet wife, Annie, went home to Heaven a few weeks ago. This Christmas Eve we would have been married five years. Words can't express how much she meant to me and what a gift from God a loving wife is. It's great when all you have to do is walk in a room and she's happy. If there's any kind of problem between you, you solve it as fast as you can because you feel like you're dying if there's any hurt feelings at all. You learn real quick not to sweat the small stuff and there's not much worth fighting about. At the end of the day, coming home to her you feel like you could take on the world, and before you turn out the light you pray together and you thank God for her and your marriage. You kiss her and squeeze her, and tell her you love her.

For a brief, shining moment, God blessed me with such a wife. Thankfully, I realized how lucky I was. We both did. She never needed diamonds or jewels, though I gave her some. I never needed much either…I had her. So, if you guys out there are dreaming of a big screen or a new set of clubs…sneak up behind your wife sometime and wrap your arms around her. You've already got the best gift a man can have.

I miss you, baby. If He'll allow it, pick us out a nice little cabin by a lake and when my time comes I'll be in your arms again….

So many people were so nice to us. I'm hesitant to name names for fear I'll leave someone out, but, here goes anyway. I want to say how much I appreciate my kids, Christine and William and my stepdaughter, Marie. As sweet and good as they were to Annie they buoyed me and strengthened me too. Marie's husband Mickey, and their kids were always so nice. Mickey's grandparents, Perry and his wife were so good to Annie. Jeff Dutton and the members of Victory Temple were always so good to us both. Jerry, Annie's boss, and Tammy, along with everyone at the clinic did all they could. My brothers Paul and Eddie, (Neal and Kenny, already in heaven), sisters, Lisa and Caroline, and their spouses, Jessica, Rachel, Nila, Belinda and Russ helped us so much. Everyone at the transplant clinic was so patient, compassionate and kind. Everyone at the Rite Aid where Marie works, was always so sweet to Annie.

Annie's Dad and stepmother Joan visited her often. Her sisters and her niece, Tabitha, helped a lot. I want to say also, how much I appreciate the good people I work with like Martha, Sylvia, Tammy, Cathy, Pat, Charlotte, Yvette, Velvet, Marc, Jane, Brenda, Sheila, Clifton, David, Mark, Gary, Dean, Stephen, Sid, Suzanne, Stan, Rick, Jeff, Brenda, Vicky, Rose, Cowboy Shane, the Duke of Rand-El and Glenda. Their kindness and prayers meant a lot while Annie was so sick and the hard time after she died.

My friends, Stanton Erwin, Mickey Pass and Larry Black prayed with me and cried with me several times. Lula Mae Harris prayed for Annie and me. My good friends Billy Johnson and Jim Jackson never said much but they were there to look me in the eye and shake my hand. Paul and Tim Askew, Fletcher Helms, Fred Nesbitt, Margaret Davis, C.J. Blalock, Ed Clark and my aunt Jean Johnson have always been good to me. Karen Satterfield had to work harder while I was out and I appreciate her. Greg and Beth Masters fed William many times while he visited their son, Parks, while I was out of town with Annie. William's buddy, Luke Baldridge was always good for some humorous distraction if he was staying here with William. The same goes for Jody Hyde, Tab Fowler, Jimmy Little, and Glenn Moyer as well as Luke and Parks for being such good friends to William and mine too.

Christine's friends, Ashley and Amanda were so sweet and Christine's boyfriend, now husband, Kenny, was good to her, and to Annie and me.

Dr. Baker took Annie's braces off shortly before she died. I remember Annie running her tongue over her smooth teeth and smiling so sweetly, excited at how pretty her smile was, so weak she could barely walk. The old doctor in Atlanta was so good to Annie.

My Girl

My doctors, Dr. Brent Box and Brenda Fisher took good thoughtful care of me.

It seems when you're walking a walk like this you're all alone in the world, but you're not. Every person that gives you a kind word or a pat on the back keeps you going. Every prayer, every chicken casserole and every tear keeps you going. I'm saying thanks for every act of kindness that so many showed to us while we were walking through that gauntlet and to me after Annie died. If I missed someone and I'm sure I did, I'm sorry, my memory isn't what it used to be. I turned fifty about a month ago.

Most of all I want to thank my parents Ken and Poncy, for showing me how good life can be by loving each other and honoring God in their marriage and in their home. Even more so I want to thank the Lord for so richly blessing me for the brief time I had with Annie and the friends and family that loved us both. I guess her life was a lot like that shooting star we saw that night, dazzling and wonderful, but all too brief.

Her stone is on a hillside buried a stone's throw from my parents. Engraved on it are the words from the song she sang in church that day, "Yes, Lord, yes. To Your will and to Your way. Yes, Lord, yes I will trust You and obey…"

Epilogue

Bobby Nicholson is living with his son Curtis and his family in Tennessee. He earned a Purple Heart, Silver Star, and Bronze Star for his service in Korea fighting in battles like "Pork Chop Hill". He still reads his Bible and enjoys his sons, their wives, and his grandkids. He works in the garden as much as he can. He thinks about his dear Jeanette everyday.

I married again a year ago. Annie told me before she died I'd need someone and that she understood. She was right. Annie just left too big a hole in me.

My Girl

I met a sweet, fabulous girl named Jana who teaches fifth grade and has a teenage daughter named Hannah Jo and a little boy named Jake. My daughter Christine just got married and works as a registered nurse in Alabama. My son William is in his second year at Kennesaw State, making mostly A's. I see Annie's girl, Marie, and her family often. Annie's son Derek has three little girls now. The youngest is named Annie.

Printed in the United States
104173LV00001B/223-225/P